Luis Pástor Villalobos

Riding The Bus 2
The Sequel

Luis Pástor Villalobos

Copyright © 2012 Luis Pastor Villalobos

All rights reserved.

ISBN:
ISBN-13: 978-1484836897

DEDICATION

I would like to dedicate this book to the miracle of life. Before I thank anyone I must first thank my God who has given me the courage to ride the bus and to write on the bus. I want to thank my wife, my son, my daughter, my students, my colleagues, friends and the countless people I meet on the bus and on the road. You are all truly my inspiration.

ACKOWLEDGEMENTS

Although I say that
my poetry is not necessarily for
Christians, just as the Holy Bible is at the
reach of anyone's hands, I have to acknowledge that
without Jesus in my life I would not have been able to
publish my second book of free-verse story poems. I also
want to acknowledge my son, daughter, my wife and my
extended family. I want to acknowledge the inspiration that I
have received from my students and thank them for enriching
my life. Lastly, I have to acknowledge the countless awesome
people I meet when I am on public transportation and on the
road. Thank you all for being the reason I write.

□□□

CONTENTS

	Preface	xvii
	Highlights	xxi
	Before you embark	xvii
1.	**"Fun" Raising (1)**	
2.	**4/4/4 (2)**	
3.	**7/11 (3)**	
4.	**Always Thinking (4)**	
5.	**Backseat Driver (5)**	
6.	**Band-aide (6)**	

Big Person (7)	7.
Bonding (8)	8.
Born To Be A Winner (9)	9.
By The Window (10)	10.
Cheaper By The Dozen (11)	11.
Dollar Drive (12)	12.
Door # 21 (13)	13.
Fanny Pack (14)	14.
First Day (15)	15.
Forgive Spain (16)	16.
Forgive The USA (17)	17.
Forgiveness (18)	18.
Garbage (19)	19.
Get Up (20)	20.
Getting A Ride (21)	21.
Going Long, Again (22)	22.

Good Memories (23)	23.
Happy Father's Day (24)	24.
Have A Nice Day (25)	25.
He Forgave Her (26)	26.
His Legacy (27)	27.
Hope (28)	28.
How Long? (29)	29.
How To Have Sex (30)	30.
How Will You Fight? (31)	31.
I Am A Dreamer (32)	32.
I Declare His Salvation (33)	33.
I Feel Good (34)	34.
I Got Punished (35)	35.
I know (36)	36.
I Want To Be Stupid (37)	37.
I Was Wrong (38)	38.

I'll Show You (39)	39.
If Somebody wants... (40)	40.
It Goes Fast (41)	41.
It Started (42)	42.
It Was Meant To Be (43)	43.
It's Easy (44)	44.
Laughing Man (45)	45.
Laundry Bus (46)	46.
Like A Dog (47)	47.
Make Girls Cry (48)	48.
Massage On The Bus (49)	49.
Mi Limo (50)	50.
Mi Mami (51)	51.
Missing The Bus (52)	52.
Music On The Bus (53)	53.
New Faces (54)	54.

No (55)	55.
No Feet (56)	56.
Now I Know (57)	57.
Oh Really? (58)	58.
One Free One (59)	59.
One Good Fight (60)	60.
One One (61)	61.
Only Once In A Lifetime (62)	62.
Paying Attention (63)	63.
Piano For Cleaning (64)	64.
Picking tomatoes (65	65.
Priceless (66)	66.
Procrastination 2 (67)	67.
Quiet (68)	68.
RDD (69)	69.
Recycling Bus (70)	70.

Red, Green, Yellow (71)	71.
Relaxing (72)	72.
Riding High (73)	73.
Riding The Bus 2 (74)	74.
Rise (75)	75.
Shape Of A Gun (76)	76.
She Cried (77)	77.
Sign Of The Cross (78)	78.
Silent (79)	79.
Sitting On A Bench (80)	80.
Sleeping On The Bus (81)	81.
Snoring (82)	82.
Son At The Bus Stop (83)	83.
Student On The Bus (84)	84.
Survive/Thrive (85)	85.
Take The First (86)	86.

The Morning (87)	87.
The Two D's (88)	88.
The World Is My Home (89)	89.
Time To Part (90)	90.
Time, My Best Friend (91)	91.
Tree (92)	92.
Trusting (93)	93.
Two Choices (94)	94.
Under Construction (95)	95.
Wetbacks (96)	96.
What Can You See? (97)	97.
What Ever It Takes (98)	98.
Why Worry? (99)	99.
Woman Singing (100)	100
You Can Do All Things (101)	101
You Will Go Far (102)	102

Preface

My series of Riding Bus 1 – saving money, dreams and inspiration; Riding The Bus 2 – *The Sequel*; Riding The Bus 3 – *the dream continues*; Andar en Autobus; Prendre l'autobus; and Riding The Bus - *with Jesus* are nothing more than miracles! When I started writing poetry on the bus I often would share my poems with my students and it was they who told me that I should publish a book. While some students joke about my poems, down deep inside I know that they become moved to try to improve and many have told me that they have been inspired. Likewise, people of all ages and walks of life have shared with me their admiration of my poetry. Sincerely, it is I who admire them for being my inspiration.

Many who have heard, read my poems or bought my first book have shared with me that they identify with my stories. My book is not about my life experiences but those of all people in one way or another. We all know a homeless person, perhaps a family member. We all have not had perfect lives. What is important is not that we struggled but that we traveled the road courageously. If you are going through difficult times at this moment, don't stop, keep going and get out!

In Riding The Bus 2 – *The Sequel* I will continue the tradition of sharing my life experiences and observations of people and life. I will not only talk about my observations on the bus but also of my students, my family and my life. I will not limit myself to secular subjects but I will also share my faith in God in a candid way because God is a part of my life and I cannot exclude Him. I hope that "Riding The Bus – saving money, dreams and inspiration" and the following poems in "Riding The Bus 2 – *The Sequel"* will continue to inspire you to go onto the next level as my poems have inspired me.

I am very proud to inform you that I am now beginning my third year of riding the bus and I have made great economic advances. In addition to my regular monthly credit card payments, I have paid over 16,000 dollars of debt just by riding the bus. I am very proud to say that this month I finished paying all my debt with the exception of my mortgage. Now I am going to begin saving six times my monthly income as I advice in my first book. Riding the bus has given me a view of how other people live and the tremendous amount of poverty there is in our communities. I am committed to getting completely out of debt and never use credit again. I want to be economically fit to help my family and the community without having to worry about my own needs.

One more note: like Riding the bus 1, Riding The Bus 2 also introduces every poem with a short paragraph depicting the moral, reflection or message behind the poem. Many readers have shared with me that they like my style of giving direction to the reader before the poem is read. So no, there are not two poems on the same page, only one. Nevertheless, let your imagination be your guide.

Riding The Bus 2 – *The Sequel*

Luis Pástor Villalobos

Highlights

It is difficult to highlight any particular poem. When looking at any of my poems, each one seems to have some unique feature that will make it stand out. Even the poems that I feel are not very profound have the potential to speak to any particular person. Therefore, allow me to highlight concepts such as gratitude and positive thinking. Overall, my poetry sends the message of resilience in spite of all circumstances.

For example, in my first book Riding The Bus 1, my poem "I have feet" merely shows gratitude, the fact that we have feet to walk. Sometimes the challenges of life blind our eyes to the simple things in life. One might conclude then that having no feet would be detrimental. In my poem "No feet" I offer the idea that one can be happy even without feet. Nick Vujicic, a man born without arms and legs, lives a life that many would be astonished to learn. Please watch "No arms, no legs, no worries" on YouTube and you will see how positive thinking can make all the difference.

Another common theme throughout my poetry is finances. Saving money is unheard of for most Americans. It is said that most Americans barely have 500 dollars in their savings. People use credit like candy and fall deeper and deeper into debt. We have been sold the lie that we can have anything we want through credit. In Riding The Bus 1, I dedicated a poem to Chase Bank. In my first book I explain how I was dozing off on the bus and woke up to a sign that said "Chase Bank". I would like to think that God spoke to me in that instance. I proceeded to sell my Toyota Tacoma and used that money to pay off my wife's van which left me with 700 dollars per month, money I began using on the road to debt freedom.

In my poem "Chase Bank" in Riding The Bus 1, I play with the word "chase" and essentially tell the bank to stop chasing me and my money. I was determined to pay off all my credit cards and eventually pay off my house and live debt free. In Riding The Bus 2, I continue my quest to show people that being debt-free is the best way to go. The poem "Riding High" is also a lively play of words. The word "high" can refer to a level in the bus, a style of life and also a state of being intoxicated. In my poem all three are exposed: "high" because my son and I were sitting at the back of the bus, the highest level; "high" because I felt like a rich/smart man who was spending his money wisely; "high" because the young man a few seats behind us was smoking recreational cannabis. Clearly, spending money wisely can be a lot of fun. ☐☐☐

Let's talk about forgiveness for a while and let's cross-reference it to the victim mentality. As I grew up in school, especially high school and college I learned about the Westward Expansion, Eminent Domain and Manifest Destiny. Along with the Mecha Club and Chicano studies in college I learned to resent the dealings of Anglo-Saxons with natives of a land we now call America, the conquista by the Spaniards of Mexico and many other peoples and conquered lands. I developed an unrest that is prevalent among people we refer to as minorities or people with darker skin. Many feel that they have been stripped of their identity. In my poem "Forgive The USA" I acknowledge the evil that has been committed but at the same time I know that the US may be the best country to achieve goals, especially for the poor and the underdog. "Forgive Spain" is the recognition that there is a way of looking at things from a different perspective. If society begins to say "I forgive you and I'm sorry, please forgive me" we are going to be better, a people enriched by two cultures. Lastly, if you can't forgive yourself, you won't be able to forgive those who have offended you. "Forgiveness" entertains the idea that forgiving others is where true freedom lies. Nobody is perfect, no country, no system. We have to aspire to work together for the betterment of all.

If I had to describe my poetry in two words, it would be positive thinking. Positive thinking encompasses all those other concepts like hope, love, faith... In my poem "Two choices" I capitalize on the idea that positive thinking is the only way to go. Life is a series of good and bad choices and our actions will determine the final outcome. If you want something you have to work at it. "Born to be a winner" is not about bragging about myself. I denote many of the goals that I have accomplished and I still dream of things to come. Throughout all life's struggles we have to maintain a positive outlook in spite of challenges and reassure ourselves that things will get better if we don't give up. This poem clearly shows that I appreciate the things I have accomplished and keep my options open for more good things to come.

Another subject I touch upon often in my poetry is my honest feelings about God. It is not my quest to discuss theology, to trash other religions and I am not trying to prove anything, because I can't. My sole belief in God is based on faith, hope, love, compassion, empathy, feelings and convictions that should not be refuted. I chose to give

God a name and call Him Jesus, principally because it is recorded in the Bible that He was crucified and died on the cross for the sins of the world, rose again on the third day and now I have the hope that I will be with Him some day in heaven. My poem "His legacy" talks about my paternal father's relentless efforts to make me a Bible-believing Christian. I think he accomplished his goal. Now I can't stop talking about God to my children. In my poem "I Declare His Salvation" I allude to a teaching of the church that when one member of a family is saved then all other family members will follow. Also, salvation is not something that can be enjoyed only in heaven, but one can begin to experience a better life style here in earth.

Family is extremely important in my life. I always dreamed of having a loving wife and children. While there are probably no perfect families in the world it is most people's aspirations to have the best family possible. Through my poetry I have several poems dedicated to my son, daughter and wife. The main message in those poems is that I love my family. "Make girls cry" is a boost for my son to keep his ground no matter the circumstances. Sometimes children can be the most cruel when dealing with their counterparts. "The two d's" stand for daughter and dad. As my daughter grew older we grew apart but the day came when she needed me again and my heart was renewed. Lastly, a husband has to love his wife and that too is not an easy task. Relationships require work to make them work. "How will you fight?" is about love not fighting but sometimes we have to fight with love to keep the love alive. Clearly, loving family is all worth it.

Education encompasses a great part of my poetry. As a teacher I had the privilege of affecting students in positive ways. My biggest feat in education was to motivate my students especially those who were being left by the wayside. I believed in inspiring them and being real with them. I assured them that all they needed in life to be successful was themselves and the desire to succeed. As part of our warm-up I would have students do a quick-write on a poem or short video. There was a time for students to share their writing and it was during this time that I saw my students shine. "The world is my home" talks about my educational trips to Europe. Many students traveled with me to France, Spain and England and I can tell you that their lives were changed.

There is so much more I could say about Riding the bus 2 – the sequel, such as one of my favorites, "RDD" where I call racism an illness. People need to have positive dialog to heal the pain of the past. I hope that in the future racism will be identified as a social illness that will be cured with therapy perhaps medication. I could talk about my poem "Rise" that I dedicated to my migrant worker students. I am very proud to say that I too grew up as migrant farm worker. Overall, my poetry is about thinking positive, having dreams and accomplishing them.

In conclusion, I would like to challenge my readers to go over and beyond. Anything that is worth anything will require much effort. When you meet an obstacle in life make it a stepping stone. With every challenge move forward so when you look back you will see the tracks where you struggled. You will be proud of yourself when you consider where you have been, where you are today and where you are going. I was a farmworker as a child and a teen, which is a very honorable job but very badly paid.

Luis Pástor Villalobos

Before you embark

Get ready to embark on your journey through my second book of free-verse inspirational story poems. If you are familiar with my first book, Riding The Bus 1 – saving money, dreams and inspiration, you should expect similar thought-provoking stories. These story poems are based on real events experienced by me, friends, family and my observations on the bus or related to public transportation. Please enjoy my poetry and embrace your life, ready for great things to come.

Do not "sweat' through the reading of my poetry. My books are not the type that you have to read in order. You can close your eyes and open the book at any page and read one or two poems. Every page is a unit in itself, the top of the page is the beginning and the bottom of the page is the ending. All my poems are introduced with a back story that will explain origin and guide you with a message, reflection or moral. Nonetheless, you are your own guide and you will be inspired in your own unique way.

Now you are ready to embark. Your mode of transportation is your feet, wheelchair, bus, train, car, plane but more importantly, your imagination. You set your own limits, beyond the skies. You may want to try some of my suggestions, you want to stop some things, it is up to you. It is my hope though that you will grow through this experience, that you will become a better you, ready to be catapulted to the next level. ❑❑❑

Luis Pástor Villalobos

"Fun" Raising (1)

Reflection: I am very proud to say that I am working on my third educational excursion to Europe. It has not been easy; it is difficult to raise money especially during these hard economic times. A student of mine told me that the activities had to be fun to attract students and I agreed. Every year I try somethinbreak the monotony. Running a 501 (c) 3 is hard work and I wouldn't wish it upon my worst enemy, if I had one.

"Fun" Raising (1)

It is difficult to fundraise.
Long tedious hours,
People too busy to participate,
The commitment they made forgotten.

The activities have to be "fun" so that,
Students and parents will want to collaborate.
The activities must be interesting, exciting,
So that students will remember their dream.

Take the "d" out of fundraising.
To make it "fun", it's not just about money,
Car washes and bake sales are overrated,
New ideas, competition, sponsorships.

Raising hopes and dreams, the commitment
To do what others consider impossible.
Going places where others are afraid to go,
"Fun" raising, learning, living the dream.

4/4/4 (2)

Message: Numbers may sometimes hold a symbolic power, although I don't hold to believe in numerology. Nevertheless, I don't think that it is a coincidence that my daughter was born on 4/4/94 and my mother died on 4/4/4. Perhaps the sole purpose of these magical numbers was to inspire the title of this poem. This story is a glimpse of the circle and miracle of life: my daughter replacing my mother. The bloodline will continue for centuries to come.

4/4/4 (2)

Bitter, sweet celebration,
It was my daughter's birthday,
A day I would never forget.

I had the cake knife in hand,
Ready to cut the first slice,
Then I received the dreadful phone call.

I put the knife down,
Like I knew what the call was about.
"Our mother has just passed, she sobbed."

It had been months since,
My mother was terminally ill,
Thought I should have cancelled the party.

"My mother has just passed", I announced.
"No one can tell me I can't leave."
A celebration of life and death.

7/11 (3)

Message: Teaching may be the kind of job that requires a part-time job or some kind of supplemental income. Many teachers opt to do something on the side to afford the life style of their neighbors. In this poem you will see teachers boasting of their second income to make ends meet. Someday I hope to boast that I am a renowned author of a series of "Riding The Bus" books.

7/11 (3)

It was the end of a tough week of work,
Sitting at a table with three other teachers,
I observed them exchange dialogue.

"I have a couple of houses,
The renters are behind and I have to go collect,
It's such a headache to have a second job."

The second teacher says, "I have a couple of,
Investments I have to monitor,
When I get home I have to check my books."

The third bragged about his restaurant,
"I make twice as much as my teacher's salary,
As soon as I can, I'm out of here!"

I know what you mean I interjected, "I have to,
Go home to take care of my seven eleven,
They were amazed, "You have a seven eleven!?
"Yea, my son is 7 and my daughter 11.

Being a good father is like a second job.

Always Thinking (4)

Message: Riding the bus has given me time, just to think. I do not have to pay attention to the steering wheel, use my peripheral vision or glance at the rear view mirror. All I have to do is follow my dream that someday I will be known as the "bus writer" of poems, hopes and dreams. If you have a goal in life you cannot give up even if the road looks bleak. The real winners in life are those who keep going in spite of all the obstacles.

Always Thinking (4)

I don't know,
Where all these words
Are coming from,
Actually, I do.

I barely finished,
Publishing my first book,
And I am already writing,
The sequel to "Riding The Bus 1"

The words just keep coming,
And they won't stop,
I'm reliving the past,
Foretelling the future.

All in the present,
My LUCKY PEN keeps going,
The thoughts coming,
Always thinking.

I am now writing, on the bus.

Backseat Driver (5)

Message: Like I said before, there are all kinds of people on the bus. Sometimes a child can catch the attention of others better than an adult. The boy highlighted in this poem had the gift of imagination. He was not inhibited by the people who were observing his ability to drive the bus all the way from the back seat. His father nevertheless seemed quite annoyed by his creativity.

Backseat Driver (5)

The smartest people in the world are,
Children, and I can prove it to you.
Children can imagine anything and everything.
No bars held when it comes to imagination.

A four year old at the back of the bus,
Is driving the bus like an expert.
He brakes, accelerates, the engine roaring,
Back seat driver catches everyone's attention.

The father seemed to be annoyed,
Asking his son several times to settle down.
The boy obviously did not stop,
He continued to drive from the back.

I had to intervene and compliment,
"Your son is very intelligent", I said.
Children have a great imagination,
They have the ability to change the world.

Band-aide (6)

Message: Sometimes when I remember my brother Manuel my heart becomes filled with sorrow. He is such an intelligent man with so much potential but his abusive past alcohol and drugs have taken hold of his life. During the fall of the economy and the security scare in the U.S. he was deported to Mexico and denied his legal status due to his mile-long record with the police.

Band-aide (6)

I think this is really funny,
This is truly profound,
My brother's VW was rear-ended.
The van was in need of a band-aide.

Who would have thought?
My brother literally took wood,
Drilled holes, sanded and painted,
A large band-aide and affixed it on the back.

Now this story gets more profound,
My brother is and always was intelligent,
But a neglected and abusive childhood,
Has led him to a style of homelessness.

Yes, it gets even more deep,
What if someone could build,
A giant band-aide to cover my brother's pain,
And the ailments of the world?

Big Person (7)

Message: This is a very special poem about my high school French teacher. She was instrumental in my becoming a French teacher. She became a very special friend who listened to my problems. In some cases she showed more concern for my life than I did for myself. She was one of those people who supplemented the love that was missing in my home.

Big Person (7)

A person's size is not,
The measure of his greatness,
It is the size of the heart,
The willingness to care for others.

My high school French teacher,
Was a little person, less than 4 feet,
But her love for her students,
Was twelve feet high.

She was my mentor, my counselor,
My friend, my confidant.
When I couldn't stand it at home,
I would spend the weekend with her.

We would speak nothing but French,
She was an awesome cook,
She helped me to organize,
My trip to France in my senior year.

Do you need to be big?
To do things for people?
To help those in need? The measure,
Of your greatness is your service.

Bonding (8)

Reflection: Having goals and dreams require much effort. My daughter and I are both tenacious beings who won't give up or waver from our goals. She is now at her dream school, Parsons The New School and I am months away from publishing my second book. We both have worked sleepless nights trying to finish projects that ran into the night. We are still working hard: she with her dream to be a successful fashion designer and me with my dream to be a renowned book author.

Bonding (8)

My daughter was stressed out,
Six page essay due the next day, thought
She wouldn't stay awake through the night,
I offered to stay up with her.

Side by side, she on her laptop,
I, on mine working on my website,
My dream to become a writer,
My daughter's dream to get a 4.0.

Bonding, working toward a common goal,
Confirming that dreams come true,
Through hard work and dedication,
Never giving up in spite of the odds.

Finally my eyes begin to get heavy,
"Mija, I think I better get some sleep."
"It's ok dad, I'll be ok", she assured.
"I love you mija, get a little sleep ok?"

Born To Be A Winner (9)

Message: I thank God that I am different. I made decisions in life and I stayed after them. I believe we are all winners, born to accomplish goals in life. Some people reach their goals early in life and others in their later years. I am not finished with my goals yet. I have many more dreams to follow; I will be finished when I am laid to rest.

Born To Be A Winner (9)

Out of seven brothers and sisters,
I am the only one who can swim,
The only one who has published a book,
The only one who is trilingual.

Out of seven brothers and sisters,
I am the only one who has traveled to Europe,
The only one trained in martial arts,
The only one who raps educational songs.

I was born to be a winner,
Out of seven children the only one,
Who has visited the pyramids of Mexico,
El Zócalo, Chichén Itzá, Teotihuacán.

I was born to be different,
The only one who rides the bus,
The only one to write poems,
Will I also be, the only millionaire?

By The Window (10)

Message: I believe in miracles and I think that the purchase of my current house was a total miracle. I was on a waiting list for two years until the price of the house I wanted declined and I was able to afford it. When I used to drive to work I would often get sleepy, park my Perpetual Giver (my Toyota Tacoma, see my first book) and I would take a nap in front of the house that is now mine. I never lost hope of my dream to own a brand new, two-story home. Dreams really do come true and the best is yet to come: total debt freedom.

By The Window (10)

Sometimes I like to sit down,
On my grandfather chair by the window.
Looking out, I remember when,
I used to park in front of my house,
When the house was not yet mine.

I would sit in my car,
Glance at the sign that said "PENDING"
I would pray, "God if you want,
This house will be mine."

Now I am in the inside looking out.
I pray and thank God for the miracle.
Who would have thought,
That my dream would come true?

Now I am still praying and dreaming,
Hoping that I will stay at my house,
And say that it is totally mine.
Three years is the planned payoff date.

Now, I think I'll take a short nap.

Cheaper By The Dozen (11)

Message: This mother of twelve is going to stay in my thoughts for years to come. As a teacher I have seen several students fall to the wayside, as this woman's son. Many of these students are talented and have the potential to accomplish much in life. Recently her son moved to Arizona, got away from bad company and started a new life, taking with him my poem and my special gift.

Cheaper By The Dozen (11)

Remember I told you,
You see all kinds of people on the bus?
Children, students, the elderly, single,
Married, divorced, single mothers...

Then I met a woman with 12 children,
She spoke highly of all of them,
All successful and doing well,
With the exception of one.

He hooked up with the wrong crowd,
He cut school for months,
Without any notification from his school,
Lost so many credits, finally dropped out.

It's cheaper by the dozen,
Twelve eggs in a carton,
Twelve pack of beverages,
Many other products are sold by the dozen,

Blessings should also come by the dozen,
"I pray that you bless the twelve
Especially the one that went astray.
Lord, wipe the tears from his mother's eyes."

Dollar Drive (12)

Message: One of the biggest fundraisers EFIST has had is to simply go from house to house, business to business, person to person asking for just one dollar, the dollar most people will play on the Lotto at one point or another. Some play extensive Lotto and they visit the local casinos as well. People seem to get a thrill at trying to win something from sheer luck. I propose a sure way to win. Give to our youth. Thank you.

Dollar Drive (12)

"Hello, I am Luis Villalobos,
The president of EFIST International,
(a designated 501 (c) 3 corporation),
Designed for international student travel".

"We are coming to the community
To ask for your support,
Not 5, not 10, 15, 20 or 25 dollars,
Just one little dollar".

"Many people, especially poor people,
Will spend 5 dollars on the Lotto,
If you give us just one dollar,
You are sure to be a winner".

"Invest in our youth,
They need you, your contribution,
Give a young kid a chance,
And he will show you the world!"

Door # 21 (13)

Message: Hard work and tenacity always pays off. I don't know what got into me at such an early age, I just wanted to succeed. I was going to do the right thing. I was not going to join gangs, take drugs and steal like others in my community. I was going to be different. I knew this at a very early age. Today I am still working hard and tenacity is still paying off.

Door # 21 (13)

I was 10, my father had a big fight,
And he went back to Mexico.
My mother was left alone to fend for us.

Something inside me moved me,
Not to be conformed,
With my current situation.

I took to the streets,
Walked across the tracks,
Where the rich kids lived.

I knocked on doors,
Gave them my sad story.
"I am poor, I have no father,
I want to go to college when I grow up.

Maybe 20 doors,
Were shut on my face,
But when I got to door 21,
Raked some leaves, hearty meal,
And walked home with a smile.

Fanny Pack (14)

Message: People seem to make fun of men who wear fanny packs. It seams that fanny packs carry the stereotypical female fanny pack. I started wearing my fanny pack since my first excursion to Europe and I never took it off since. Like my LUCKY PEN, my fanny pack has become a symbol of who I am. I have made the commitment to take teens on educational excursions.

Fanny Back (14)

"Is that a fanny pack?", I was asked.
It was evident, they were looking at it.
My fanny pack, a symbol of me.

Both buttocks, firmly planted,
No thick wallet throwing of my balance,
Me, buttocks, bus seat united.

Lucky Pen, never to get lost,
School keys, flash drive connected.
Can't walk off without them.

My fanny pack, a belt,
To hold up my pants,
A man standing in the face of danger.

Next time you want to poke fun,
At a man wearing a fanny pack,
Remember me, the tough guy.

First Day (15)

Reflection: Starting something new can be difficult. Expectations can be high and low all at the same time. What is important is to keep going, always expecting that life will be better. Only time will tell what will happen. If we don't give up, everything will be fine in the end. So don't give up, keep working toward your goal as if it was the first day all over again.

First Day (15)

Fear, confidence,
Expectations, surprises, doubts,
Hope, all mixed in one.

The first day of school,
The first day after the wedding,
The first day I hold my child.

What will happen this year in school?
What will my marriage be like?
How will my children turn out?

The first day, the first time,
Difficult and easy all in one,
What should I do first, second, third?

Soon the last day will come,
Just as the first day came,
To reflect on what was or could have been.

Forgive Spain (16)

Message: Forgiveness is essential if you want to move forward. Too many people hold grudges against people of the past. We forget that not everyone is the same and that people change. Europe has become a multicultural land just like anywhere in the world. In Europe people of all colors, race and cultures speak multiple languages. I think it is important that we remember the good things to help us forgive.

Forgive Spain (16)

Since I started organizing,
Educational trips to Europe,
I have visited Spain twice.
I have kept a friend from Spain,
For more than five years.

I forgive Spain for conquering Mexico,
I forgive Spain for mistreating the natives,
I discovered that Spaniards are like,
Anyone else in the world.
They get angry, cry and get happy.

I forgive myself for holding,
Grudges against people of the past.
Today I seek out everywhere,
The good in every culture, like my friend,
Who sees past the color of the skin.

Forgive the history of a race of conquerors,
Forget the struggle and remember the dream,
We Hispanics have what it takes,
To go beyond our wildest dreams,
A people enriched by two cultures.

Forgive The USA (17)

Reflection: By no means is this an attack on the United States. This is my country since the age of ten and now I am a citizen through naturalization. I owe what I am today to this great country. In spite of its flaws it is still the greatest country in the world where anyone can find success. I am proud to be a naturalized American.

Forgive The USA (17)

You know, if you live your life,
Blaming others for your mishaps,
If you blame your country, family,
You won't get very far in life.

I grew up with extreme rejection,
For being Mexican-American and Korean.
In Mexico I was bullied and in the U.S.
I discovered that White kids could be cruel too.

My parents brought us here,
For a better life, against my will.
I always wondered what life would have been,
Would I have the same measure of success?

I forgive the U.S.A. for not accepting me,
For treating me like an outsider, an alien,
But here is where I became successful,
Now I can only say, "I love the U.S.A."

Forgiveness (18)

Message: If you want to have peace there is only one choice and that is to forgive. It feels so good to say or think "I don't hate you". Hate hurts you and destroys your own life. There is no better gift than to forgive someone. Remember that sometimes people hurt each other without intention. Nobody is perfect, so forgive yourself and others.

Forgiveness (18)

It is such a good feeling,
To finally say, "I forgive you".
You set yourself free,
From the shackles of hate.

Say, "I forgive you",
To the father who left you.
Even though he can't hear,
It will be healing to your soul.

Say, "I forgive you",
To the mother who neglected you,
Who worked ten hours a day,
And you were forced to care for yourself.

Say, "I forgive you", to your country,
Your community, your neighborhood, brother,
You'll be able to think clearly,
Pick up where you left off.

Most importantly say, "I forgive you",
To yourself. Neither are you to blame.
If you cannot forgive yourself,
You will not be able to forgive others.

Garbage (19)

Reflection: When plastic products first came into existence it was customary to throw plastic material into the general garbage. Today the recycling industry has grown to the millions. People have become more aware of the efforts to conserve the earth's natural resources. What was once garbage, today is the treasure of the homeless and of the very rich. At first glance my comp book was garbage. For me, it was another one of my treasures.

Garbage (19)

I have heard people say,
"One man's garbage is
Another man's treasure."
Anything can be a treasure.

I once had a lucky pen,
For almost three years,
A lucky folder where,
I wrote things that had to happen.

Now I need a lucky notebook,
Where I can write my plans and goals.
This is my lucky comp book.
You're looking at it.

It was once mistaken for garbage,
I dug through two large bags,
Digging for dreams and miracles,
I dug until I got lucky.

Get Up (20)

Message: It is very easy to become discouraged and it's hard to continue especially when things are not going as expected. My book is not selling as fast as I thought. This coming year I will be making less due to the loss of my auxiliary class and 10 furlough days. I know I have to keep trying. I just have to keep writing poems publishing books and the rest will take care of itself.

Get Up (20)

Depression has been lurking,
I lost my lucky pen,
My first book is not selling,
Sometimes I miss the comfort of my car.

Get up! Start moving forward again.
Start dreaming again,
Be true to your own words.
Remember, never give up.

This is my first poem in two months,
Enough feeling sorry for myself,
I knew it wouldn't be easy,
Get up and walk again!

Get up again! Aren't you the one,
Who wrote the poem, Nine Times?
Even if your book doesn't sell,
Let the pen be the last to fall.

Getting A Ride (21)

Message: Being a bus rider has shown me what it is like to be on the other side. I have developed a special appreciation for both riding and driving. When I ride, I can write, sleep and relax. When I drive, although I can't do any of the above, generally I arrive to my destination a little faster. I appreciate it so much when someone sees me walking and picks me up.

Getting A Ride (21)

When I used to drive,
I would often give rides,
To people who were less fortunate.

I never accepted monetary compensation,
For offering my transportation services,
Now I am being paid back.

Now that I am riding the bus,
Countless people and friends,
Offer to pick me up or drop me off.

They don't accept a few dollars,
For a ride here and there,
I am very grateful to them all.

Now that I ride I know how it feels,
To wait for a half hour,
For a bus that never showed.

Going Long, Again (22)

Message: It is easy to give up and many of us do give up on many of our goals. I believe what is important is not whether we won or lost, but that we tried. I am going to grow my hair long again, apply hair products to try to save it. I am going to keep trying to become a well-known writer and I will keep trying to build an army of French-Speaking soldiers who will pass the AP French test.

Going Long, Again (22)

My hair has been falling off lately,
My students are not working,
To their fullest potential,
But I shouldn't give up on them or me.

My book is not selling,
The way I thought it would sell,
We lost the Home Coming game,
But I'm going long again.

My hair is short again
A fresh new start,
My second book is coming out,
I am not giving up.

2014, 18 students scheduled
To pass the AP French test,
Paris, Madrid and Rome,
Awaiting to celebrate the victory!

Good Memories (23)

Reflection: Every bad situation has a silver lining. Sometimes it is hard to see the good in things, but if we wait, the day will come. This dear friend was worthwhile waiting for. It is interesting that among all bad memories, one very good one would stand out. I am so grateful to my friend, his wife and their son, my student.

Good Memories (23)

Difficult times, those days, awaiting
I walked into church rather depressed,
Then I saw his gesture, waving,
To come and sit next to him and his family.

The wave of his had assured me,
That things would get better,
Soon I moved away,
And parted from my past.

Fate would have it though,
That I would see him again,
Walking in the mall with my son,
And he walking with his son, my student.

I saw my past approaching,
Smiling at me from afar,
Glad I met up with him again,
His friendship to keep for years to come.

Happy Father's Day (24)

Message: The public bus is filled with people of all walks of life. Some are professionals, others day laborers, some are homeless and others are emotionally disturbed. In this gamut of personalities one can find the greatest contrasts. A stranger greeted me at the bus stop and continued to greet others while a boy suffers the insults of his mother.

Happy Father's Day (24)

It has been a little over a year,
Since I sold my perpetual giver,
I don't remember last year's celebration,
But this year will be memorable.

Breakfast at I-HOP and church,
All of us receiving the grandest gift,
Not a brand new car, brand new stuff,
My son starts high school, daughter off to college.

Hours later my son and I at the bus stop,
A man approaches me and extends his hand,
And greets me with a Happy Father's Day.
We board the bus, a woman screaming obscenities,

What a contrast life can be,
A woman addressing a boy with obscenities,
A man greeting everyone with a Happy Father's Day,
Now, I am wishing you a Happy Father's Day.

Have A Nice Day (25)

Message: It is really nice to meet nice people, people who go out of their way to wish you a good day. Bus drivers are individuals who have the opportunity to practice polite manners. The driver in this poem took his time to bid me well. He reminded me of many other drivers who not only ignored their customer but seemed eager to argue with them.

Have A Nice Day (25)

There are all kinds of people,
All kinds of teachers, students,
Lawyers, counselors, bus drivers.

They are all human and have,
Their own unique personalities,
Some are nice, some are rude.

Some are professional, quiet,
Some friendly, with a smile,
Others scold you like a child.

"Have a good day", the driver says,
As I walk down the stairs,
"You too, thank you." I replied.

I remembered the times I've met,
Drivers who were just in a bad mood.
Thank God for nice bus drivers!

He Forgave Her (26)

Moral: Forgiveness is a tough issue, but it is the only way to go. People who hold grudges not only hurt others but they hurt themselves. Hate is stronger than chains to break. Only love is strong enough to break the harm that hate brings. I challenge you to get help and forgive others; you will save yourself. Don't wait too long or you may also lose yourself.

He Forgave Her (26)

He finally forgave her.
What else could he do?
What else should he do?
Forgiveness set him free.

What horrible things she did,
He would rather keep confidential,
But if you can think of something,
Horrendous, not far from the truth.

He finally forgave her.
He was robbed of his innocence,
He endured great distress.
In the end he came out ahead.

He finally forgave her.
He rid himself of the guilt,
The other siblings still hold grudges,
They are bound to the past.

If somebody hurts you,
Forgive that person and his deeds,
Your soul will be set free,
You'll inherit healing and success.

His Legacy (27)

Message: When people die they should leave more than just money, they should leave a legacy. In my first book I shared in one of my poems that my father came to the U.S. with his hope in his arms. He heard that schools, the economy and the style of life was much better here. I guess no one told him of the dangers of the inner-city and juvenile delinquency. Of seven children, I am the only college graduate; yet in all this he maintained that God was good and great.

His Legacy (27)

My father did not leave me money,
I did not inherit possessions,
He was not a man of great repute.
My father did not have investments,
I had to pay to cremate him,
He could not even afford to die.

My father did not leave me millions,
He left me his rich faith in God,
A failed man, with unfailing faith.
His legacy: his respect for God,
To the point of boredom,
He spoke, boasted of a great God.

Now I understand my inheritance,
The power to believe, to have faith,
During good and bad times.
His legacy eternal in nature,
Had he left me money, I couldn't keep it,
When I pass away, his legacy will pass on.

Hope (28)

Moral: I am a high school teacher so I am often a witness to drug abuse. I tell my students that drugs are something they are going to have to quit some day so they might as well quit now. Many people don't understand that the real problem is not drug addiction but addiction to one's problems. People may drink or take drugs thinking they will alleviate the problem but it will only get worse. Get professional help for those things that are wearing you down.

Hope (28)

Hope, there is always hope.
She is 14, difficult days.
Bad grades, bad relationships.

Hope says things can change.
They can get better.
And they will get better.

As long as she lives.
She can make a change.
Things can get better.

Her parents don't understand.
Her teachers don't understand.
Maybe her friends don't either.

But there is always hope.
If she makes the decision.
She can make the difference.

How Long? (29)

Reflection: We live in a society where we discard things and people we no longer want. Too many marriages end in divorce simply because the couple "grew apart". We throw away the old TV for a flat screen although the old one works fine. I believe that commitment and sacrifice are important in life. I have made a commitment to my family, students and my educational trips.

How Long? (29)

How long have you kept something?
I've kept my LUCKY PEN for 31 months so far,
I am now writing with my LUCKY PEN, on the bus.

This pen wrote the contract for ITC 2010,
It wrote the contract for ITC 2012,
The manuscript for my first book.

Imagine if you thought your wife was lucky,
Your husband, your boyfriend/girlfriend,
Your son/daughter, imagine what you could do!

They say that over 65 % of American families,
End up in divorce, neglected children, broken dreams,
How long can you keep the same wife?

How long can you keep the dream alive?
As long as it takes to make it happen?
Or will you give up before the finish line?

How To Have Sex (30)

Moral: This poem is not a satire on my friend, young people or sex. It is a story of life, how some people experience their first sexual encounter. Young people experiment in as many ways you can imagine. We all reach maturity at different levels. Some people never grow up in this subject. Sex can be very complicated.

How To Have Sex (30)

This is a weird poem.
Hormones out of control.
"Let's go to the islands", he invited,
"The prostitutes will show you,
All you need to know."

I refused. My friend and I, growing apart.
Drinking, parties, sex, fast cars.
Me? Books, bicycles, sports, work.

What did he learn? What kind of sex?
Did those girls teach him to perform?
"They will teach you how to have sex,
How to keep your wife happy in bed,"

I don't know what he learned,
His first wife left him,
At age 17, for another man.

His second wife didn't work out either,
Now he is with his third wife,
I think this one will work out.

How Will You Fight? (31)

Message: I believe that most marriages end up in divorce because they are fighting for the wrong reasons. Since communication is hard to maintain, disagreement can easily arise. A positive relationship requires work. Next time you have a problem to resolve with your spouse don't fight each other. Join forces and together fight the problem that is attacking you both.

How Will You Fight? (31)

You know, being married,
Can be a challenge,
For both hubby and "wifey".

Sometimes you just have to fight,
But how will you fight?
With love or an iron hand?

The Bibles says. "Wives
Respect your husband."
But it also says,
"Husbands love your wives."

Fight with love and conviction.
Fight to save your marriage,
Fight to communicate,
To work things out.

Remember how it was,
When you first met?
How infatuated you were?
Fight to keep the love alive.

I Am A Dreamer (32)

Message: Dreamers are people who make things happen. They believe in the impossible, thus making the impossible possible. In this poem a share with you some of the dreams that became a reality and those that are yet to come. I grieve over people who seemingly have it made in life. I grieve, for example for Lindsay Lohan, who starred in a movie called Freaky Friday where she switched rolls with her mother. It is time that Ms. Lohan become someone else, someone who dedicates her life to the service of teenagers.

I Am A Dreamer (32)

I am a dreamer,
I always was a dreamer,
I always will be a dreamer,
And I never want to wake up.

I once dreamed that,
I could be a teacher,
And today I am a teacher,
Dreaming I can be great.

I once dreamed,
I could take students to Europe,
I am doing it for the third time,
I'm dreaming and I'm not there yet.

Now I am dreaming,
That my 501 (c) 3 will be great!
That I will be sponsored,
By a celebrity, Lindsay Lohan.

I Declare His Salvation (33)

Message: I said it once and I will say it again. I believe in Jesus and I can't take Him out of my poems because I would be denying who I am. While I am riding the bus I get inspired just about anything and my pen starts going all by itself. At the same time my beliefs are not an attack on anyone else's beliefs. I share my faith in Jesus openly and candidly.

I Declare His Salvation (33)

In the Bible God makes many promises,
And I believe God keeps them all.
I claim the promise that,
My family will all be saved.

I love my wife, my son, my daughter,
If there is a heaven, I want to be there,
If there is a God, He loves them all,
Whatever it is, I want it all.

I declare his salvation now,
Right here in this life,
No poverty, prosperity for all,
No despair, instead, joy and peace.

Salvation starts now on earth,
No need to die to experience it.
My family right here and now,
Death is only life, continued on and on.

I Feel Good (34)

Message: Sometimes it is difficult to do the things we know, we are supposed to do. It was not easy for me to sell my Tacoma and I was not looking forward to riding the bus on a daily basis. Even so, I knew I had to do it and I did. When I finally did it I felt so good about myself. My Tacoma was truly mine because I was able to let it go and it was completely paid off.

I Feel Good (34)

I did what I had to do.
I let go of my pick up,
So precious to me.
A gift of God, my Toyota Tacoma.
140 miles, 5,500 dollars.

I had promised my son,
That the truck would be his,
But the economy turned on me.
Drop in earnings from 80,000 to 60,000.
No choice, I had to sell my pick up.

I feel good that I sold it.
I have to take that money,
To pay off the Town and Country.
This month, the Chrysler will be,
Completely paid off.

I feel good I sold my pick up.
When I pay off the Chrysler,
I'm going to give my wife,
The pick slip, wrapped in scarlet.
One step closer to debt freedom.

I Got Punished (35)

Message: To put it lightly, credit is a social evil. We should not own something we can't afford. Unnecessary debt destroys people, marriages and relationships. Some people learn their lesson after their first embarrassing bankruptcy. Some never learn and they end up having to downsize during their retirement years.

I Got Punished (35)

Remember I told you credit was bad?
By the time you read this poem,
You will probably be reading,
Riding The Bus 2, *The Sequel*.

I got a call allegedly from Visa,
That my APR was going to be lowered,
From 17.9 to 6.9, wow!
I called the bank to confirm.

"No, I'm sorry sir, we would never,
Make that kind of a call.
Let me assess your situation,
To see if you qualify."

I got punished, for calling my bank.
"I regret to inform you sir,
We are lowering your credit line,
From 19,000 to 11,000."

I got punished after years,
Of paying my bills on time,
Really, they did me a favor,
Thank you, no more credit.

I know (36)

Reflection: Finding the right balance in life is my greatest challenge. Trying to play my different roles is a chore. When dealing with others it is easy to pass the buck, but I think the responsibility lies at both ends. I have to believe in my students as much as they should believe in me. If you want to accomplish goals in life you should never give up, if you want to succeed.

I know (36)

I know my students are capable.
How to convince them of that fact?
Will it take a poem to motivate them?
Will it take an act of God?

I know my students are capable,
To learn much more than they realize.
How will they lose the fear of knowledge?
What will it take to produce a miracle?

What if I push them too little?
What if I push them too much?
What is the right amount of pressure,
To make them realize they can?

Perhaps they are not the problem.
Maybe I don't know I am capable,
To teach much more than I can,
Perhaps I am afraid that more will fail.

I Want To Be Stupid (37)

Reflection: Sometimes we don't like to admit we don't know something for fear of being ridiculed, or perhaps we are too proud to admit something. Whatever the case we are hurting ourselves and others by not asking for help or offering our help. I remember spending unnecessary time looking through the dictionary to find the spelling of "soliloquy". I wish someone would have helped me with my fear of being stupid during my teen years. Today, I am not afraid to ask for help.

I Want To Be Stupid (37)

Yes, that's right. If you don't admit,
That you don't know something,
Then you will not receive good advice.

If you don't know, what you don't know,
Then you will not be prepared,
To learn the things you need to learn.

First I need to discover what I don't know,
So that I can get smart in my quest to know,
I want to learn what I don't know.

The president has 12 advisors,
The principal has assistant principals,
I need to have assistants to succeed.

I want to be stupid,
So that I can get smart,
To open my mind to learn new things.

I Was Wrong (38)

Message: Until I met two fabulous students I was quite adamant about no sports in public schools. I come from a foreign country where academics is the number one attraction. Extra-curricular activities were reserved for private leagues and clubs. I was biased against students who would tell me that they needed to get a good grade in my class to stay in sports.

I Was Wrong (38)

The score was 34/44 when I arrived,
#12, #7 and #32, my students on the court.
It took a student who worked hard in class,
And hard on court to show me that I was wrong.

I understood for the first time,
The importance of sports in school.
Now, I challenge my students to play
Hard in the classroom as well.

A completed assignment is a hoop,
Turned in homework is a touchdown.
An A on a test is a goal.
Playing hard in class as well.

To make amends I will try,
To watch my students on the court,
To support them on the field,
To be there when they win.

I'll Show You (39)

Message: The evil of bullying often comes up in my poems. As a teacher I have to deal with bullying and teach against it. It seems that the more technologically advanced we become the more socially regressed we become. Bullying has invaded cyberspace and it is out of control. We shouldn't give up though, we need to teach our children to respect others no matter what.

I'll Show You (39)

It is sad that at age ten,
I felt I had to prove something.
In Tijuana I had to prove,
That I couldn't speak Chinese.

Upon coming to the U.S.
Again I had to prove,
That Mexican was my nationality,
That Spanish was my only tongue.

The children poked fun at me.
For being monolingual,
A little voice screamed inside me,
"I'll show you!"

"I will learn English so fast,
I will speak, read and write better than,
Those who are English monolinguals.
Then I will learn a third language."

"I'll show you, to poke fun at me."
It is sad that a child so young,
Be made fun of for his cultural background,
It is sad how we treat foreigners.

If Somebody Wants... (40)

Message: I believe this poem may have two messages: the power of words and seizing the opportunity. Often times people don't take opportunities for fear that they may not work. The truth is that we will never know unless we take a risk. If you think about it, it is also a risk to pass up a good opportunity. Next time you dream of the impossible, approach it with caution, perhaps with the words of a poet.

If Somebody wants... (40)

I was a freshman in college.
It was his year of retirement.
An old man with old clothing,
Walked in without saying a word.

He stared at the audience,
And the first thing he said was,
"If somebody wants to give you,
Something, talk it!"

He uttered these words,
With emotion and conviction,
A great way to introduce,
The power of poetry and words.

It took me years to really,
Grasp the power of the concept,
Now when opportunity comes knocking,
I'm not passing it away.

It Goes Fast (41)

Reflection: Time is precious. Time should be treasured and it should not be wasted. This poem is dedicated to those who know that time is worth a million dollars. Although time is endless, we humans are here on earth for a finite period. We have to make the best of our time if we want to accomplish our goals in life.

It Goes Fast (41)

"Remember the first grade?"
Two fifth grade boys were talking,
It felt like eternity for them.

I was laughing inside,
Remember the dinosaurs?
Time is immeasurable.

Every five years something major happens.
You're born, five years later you're in school.
Five more, you're an upper classman,
Five years, you're a sophomore in high school.
Five later, you're in college or married.

Now your 20 years old,
Maybe you became a parent,
Five years later, your child in school.
You see? There's no time to waste.
You see? Everything repeats itself.

I remember when I was in high school.
It seems like yesterday, in five years,
My children will be finishing college.
Five years later, I'm retired.

It Started (42)

Message: I believe that bad experiences can serve to help us appreciate life. The bad weather reminds me of those beautiful days when I walk to the bus stop early in the morning. The fresh morning air cleaning my lungs. I know life is not perfect, occasionally an old car drives by and contaminates my space. I don't dwell on that, I just hold my breath until I can breath clean air again.

It Started (42)

The bad, cold weather is finally here.
I had been forewarned of the inconvenience,
About what would happen during the rain.
Already I have gotten wet, but not soaked.

I have heard people say,
That they drive their cars,
During the cold, wet, rainy season.
Others speak of buying a rain clunker.

Will I ever buy a car again?
Yes I will, but it will be with cash.
After I pay off my debts,
I will save up for five years.

Save 500 dollars a month,
6,000 after one year,
And 30,000 in five years,
I'll have more than enough money.

In the meantime, I will buy me
Some protective clothing,
And dream of a better day.

It Was Meant To Be (43)

Reflection: Things happen for a reason. In many cases we may not know what that reason is. Something as simple as taking a different bus, driving to school, may change the course of your life. An accident or a serious illness may change your day drastically. When you miss something, don't dwell on what you lost, instead dream about what you could be gaining.

It Was Meant To Be (43)

Several times I have missed the bus,
And this is a subject that I keep touching.
Maybe because we often wonder why,
Why did I miss that bus, that opportunity?
Why did I miss this one, why that one?

Why did I marry my wife?
Why didn't I marry an old loved one?
Why am I a teacher, why?
What have I missed or gained?

I'm going to answer my own question,
The obvious answer to every question.
What is important is not what I missed,
I need to appreciate what I gained.
What would happen down a different path?

I guess it was meant to be,
To marry my wife, I love her,
I guess it was meant to be,
For me to ride this bus instead,
This poem, was also meant to be.

It's Easy (44)

Reflection: When things are easy it's no problem: people are willing to do, participate and enjoy. The will to act is quickly lost when there is a price to pay. When the weather is great we don't mind going out to enjoy the great weather. Even a little sweat after backyard work on a sunny day is great. Not so true when it is time to ride the bus on a cold, gloomy wet day.

It's Easy (44)

The weather has been great!
This summer has been really cool.
Waiting outside has been pleasant.
It's easy now to ride the bus.

But now I am wondering about winter,
When the torrent rains soak the city,
What will it be like to stand in the cold,
To have my feet wet to my ankles?

When I used to drive, I would watch people,
Run to take refuge from the rain,
I would see my students soaking wet,
Soon I will know what it's like.

It is fairly easy now, to ride the bus,
The seats are dry and comfortable,
I can work, my poems on a dry slate.
What will happen in winter? I will soon know.

Laughing Man (45)

Message: I guess this is a story about mental illness. The man highlighted in this poem could not stop laughing long enough to explain to me what was so funny. I just smiled back at him, trying to interpret his hand gestures. I saw the same man weeks later and he was still laughing. You would think that he never stopped since the last time I saw him.

Laughing Man (45)

Once again, all kinds,
Of people riding the bus.
All races, all ages, walks of life,
And now a laughing man.

Laughing hysterically,
At I don't know what.
He tried to communicate but,
I couldn't understand a word.

Laughing, talking to himself,
Smiling at people, making,
Noticeably incoherent gestures,
I wonder about people.

How did they get this way?
What are they doing?
Where are they going?
What will become of them?

Laundry Bus (46)

Message: If you ever thought you had it bad, just stop and think about others. See how the rest of the world lives. It doesn't matter if you are super rich or super poor, there is always someone who has it worse than you. Riding the bus helps me take the time to think about others. When I go out of my way to help others, my problems seem to disappear.

Laundry Bus (46)

Now I have seen it all.
A man and a woman boarded the bus,
With two humungous bags of laundry.

Wow, I thought, some people,
Have it really, really bad!
Having to carry laundry on a bus.

I thank God for my house,
On the second floor I have,
A built in washer and dryer.

The convenience of my humble abode,
I don't wish to trade with anyone,
Won't let the economy steal my home.

Money I save on the bus,
Goes straight to my mortgage.
The fallen economy will not weigh hard on me.

Like A Dog (47)

Reflection: There might be more than one lesson to this story. The man in this poem is complaining about his job instead of being thankful. The way the economy is now, any job is a good one. If you have the opportunity to go to school, do it and take it seriously. You will probably land a better paying job with more rewards and more opportunities to advance.

Like A Dog (47)

"How are you doing, sir", I inquired,
"Working like a dog", he replied.
He continued to complain about his employer.
"They work me to the bone, with little pay."

I began thinking about my life, working non-stop,
I thought of my wife, working seven days a week,
My daughter working through the night,
My son relentlessly scratching away on his violin.

I've never seen a dog work,
Much less ask for employment,
Perhaps the saying refers to homeless dogs,
Roaming the streets looking for food.

Hard work should pay off,
I alert my students by telling them,
"You should work hard toward your dream,
Or you might get caught in a dead-end street.

Make Girls Cry (48)

Message: I believe that bullying has gone out of control at a very inopportune time in society. The victim is sometimes pushed to the point of committing atrocities. During the last two decades there have been several mass shootings and almost all invariably, bullying has been a factor. I have taught my son to stay strong and only use physical force in cases of self-defense.

Make Girls Cry (48)

My son came home one day complaining,
That the bullies were calling him "gay",
For playing the violin.

"Tell them son, when I did karate,
I could make boys cry. Now that,
I play violin, I can make girls cry."

It is sad how young kids,
Can be so cruel to each other,
My son just likes to have friends,

I told my son, "They are just jealous,
Because you have a 3.8 GPA.
Because you live with both your parents.

Son if you stop playing the violin, and start getting,
Bad grades, they will tease you for not,
Playing the violin, and not getting good grades.

Massage On The Bus (49)

Message: Love can be displayed in so many ways but it was a special treat for me to see an elderly couple conducting a massage on the bus. I began to think about the 65 percent of marriages that end up in divorce. It is impressive now-a-days to see an elderly couple so involved in caring for each other, especially on a public bus. If you are married, next time your spouse has back pain, give him/her a well-deserved massage.

Massage On The Bus (49)

An elderly man and a woman boarded the bus.
The woman turned her back to her husband,
And the man began digging into her back,
Little moans and groans coming from his wife.

The elderly man must truly love his wife,
To turn my bus into a 5 star spa,
He continues to dig into her back,
With a closed fist and his knuckles.

Massage on a bus, one of a kind,
He moves to her neck and shoulders,
I became conscience of my aches and pains,
My neck, back and lower pain.

There was an empty seat across from them.
I felt like going to the man,
"Excuse me sir, how much for a massage?"
I never worked up the courage to ask him.

Mi Limo (50)

Message: Riding the bus has afforded me the opportunity to save money on transportation, reduce the stress of having to commute while driving on the freeway. I have had the opportunity to meet several interesting people and share my poetry on the bus. I feel like a rich man when I ride the bus especially when the bus is completely empty. I can close my eyes and take a nap on my way to work and home. Clearly, riding the bus has many benefits.

Mi Limo (50)

Several times I have boarded the bus,
And I was the only passenger.
I felt like a rich man in my limo,
With forty different seats to share.

I felt like telling the driver, "Go!"
My legs stretched out all the way,
My limo, line 76, the Silver Line,
My limo, stopping to pick up my friends.

Many know me, built relationships,
Supporters for my 501 (c) 3: EFIST International,
You can't have this experience,
Isolated in the comfort of your car.

My limo for only 84 dollars a month.
A savings of over 300 dollars per month,
In my limo, I am a rich man,
Who is fortunate to ride, a son of a King.

Mi Mami (51)

Reflection: When I remember my mother I have 99 percent good memories. The other 1 percent I ignore because she stayed with me the whole way through. In the Hispanic culture, the mother figure is respected. The mother often times is considered the backbone of the family. I thank God my mother was a strong woman, and her greatest quality was that she believed in the impossible.

Mi Mami (51)

Wow! What can I say about mi mami?
So many memories, so many stories, good and bad.
She went to work at 6 am and returned,
At 8 pm from the tomato-packing shed.

"Luiyo, levántame las piernas, y ponme
Unas almohadas debajo de mis piernas, por favor."
I would lift her legs, put pillows underneath,
To give her varicose veins a rest.

Most of her conversations were incoherent,
Mostly talked about what her life could have been,
But she was a wise woman too,
I listened closely to catch everything.

She once told me, "If you want to be happy,
Never fight with your wife, you will always lose".
My father seemed to fight all the time,
He never won a single fight.

Missing The Bus (52)

Reflection: I have learned to be patient about missing the bus. I have to concentrate on what I might me gaining instead of what I am missing. Missing a bus or a plane can change the course of your life. Perhaps your scheduled bus or plane was involved in an accident. Maybe you were not meant to be on that ride.

Missing The Bus (52)

It was meant to be.
I was meant to be here,
20 more minutes to think,
How life can take a different turn.
During the 911 attacks.

Some people were scheduled,
To take that perilous flight,
Due to circumstances, they missed the plane.
They lived to tell the story.
They missed something and gained another.

If you miss your bus don't worry,
You now have more time to spare.
What would have happened,
If you caught your regular bus?
What will happen when you take the next one?

Things happen because they should.
You didn't miss anything.
But you have gained everything.
If you caught your regular bus,
You would have missed all these new faces.

Music On The Bus (53)

Message: I am a musician at heart, and I can't keep still at the sound of music. I can not listen to an iPod; the music of life on the bus, on the road is much more entertaining. I enjoy talking to people, sharing my poems with strangers. Occasionally I get lucky and sell a book to a driver or a rider, which is music to my ears; "cha-ching". Occasionally, I just give a book away.

Music On The Bus (53)

Music is everywhere,
I know, I am a musician,
The pitch of the engine,
When it idles, accelerates.

The sound of the air conditioner,
Hydraulic brakes hissing at the asphalt,
Iron sharpening against iron.
The bus shaking like percussions.

Why do I need an iPod?
I can hear the rhythm
Of my seat neighbor
His ear phones blasting in my ears.

People talking, people singing,
Aloud with their music.
Children screaming, driver scolding,
Honking, the music of the bus.

New Faces (54)

Reflection: It is amazing to me how there are billions of people in the world, yet none are completely the same. The facial features, although similar, they are not the same. They are all faces with a history, with stories to tell. Missing my bus is no big deal to me because it teaches me to be patient. Besides, I love the prospect of meeting new people.

New Faces (54)

It's ok to miss the bus,
To wait another 30 minutes,
To see and meet new faces.

New faces, but the same faces.
Hispanics, Blacks, Asians, Whites,
Sad, happy, smiling, somber looks.

Different hopes and dreams,
Yet, every face like the other.
Some friendly, some angry, scorns.

I don't know what kind of problems,
These people have endured,
What triumphs they will taste.

I am riding the bus too, of course,
And people might wonder about,
My face, my story, what I do in life.

No (55)

Reflection: "No" can sometimes be a hard word to say or to hear. Since we were children we are accustomed to getting what we wanted. Unfortunately, as we grow older we find out we cannot have everything we want. Often times the things we want and get will ultimately hurt us. Don't buy on credit; save and buy cash while saving a lot on interest.

No (55)

God always answers prayers,
Sometimes he answers "no".
I don't know if I will sell,
Millions of my books.

I don't know if this poem will be,
Read by those millions of dreamers,
But I know God does miracles,
The very fact that I am alive.

God may say no temporarily,
To something we are not ready for,
No, may mean just wait a little,
Don't give up hope and faith.

If you never got what you wanted,
And God's answer is definitely no,
Rest assured. It's in your best interest,
What you want and get may destroy you.

No Feet (56)

Reflection: If you read my first book, you might remember my poem, "I have feet". In my first poem I feature something so simple: to be thankful that we have feet. In this poem I capitalize on the power of a good attitude. Throughout my life I have met people with disabilities with great attitudes and those who were distraught with their condition. I have a feeling that these people would be the same, with or without feet.

No Feet (56)

Remember that I told you,
I discovered I had feet?
What would it be like if,
I discovered I had no feet?

Sometimes people are born,
With all their limbs,
But they live out their lives,
With missing limbs.

A man boarded the bus on a wheelchair,
Had part of both legs missing,
Nicest man ever, very talkative,
Very friendly with everyone.

I never mustered up the courage,
To ask him how he lost his legs,
But if you looked at the man,
You'd think he had all his limbs.

I discovered that people,
Can be pleasant without feet,
What is important, is not what is missing,
But what you do with what you have.

Now I Know (57)

Message: The subject of missing the bus keeps coming up over and over again. This point comes often probably because it is a reminder that I am not really losing but instead gaining. In this poem you will see the obvious: that I was meant to be at the scene of this accident. I was the only one at that bus stop at that moment and I was able to help a young man that was distraught.

Now I Know (57)

Now I know,
Why I missed the bus,
I was just thinking,
That there had to be a reason.

I sat down on the bus bench,
To enjoy a beautiful morning,
I opened my laptop,
And then I heard the big bang.

I sat there for a few seconds,
And then sprung into action,
I checked the first car,
They were ok.

A badly bleeding man,
Emerged from the second car,
He was delirious.
I prayed for him, in the name of Jesus.

Now, I know.

Oh Really? (58)

Reflection: I am glad that I had this conversation with my Native-American friend. He told me the words that I needed to hear. He helped me to rid myself of the contempt of being treated like an outsider. I realize now that people are just people and the quest to acquire land has been typical of all cultures and generations, from the shores of Japan, across the Atlantic Ocean and around the world. As the world progresses and technology advances, borders will have less and less meaning.

Oh Really? (58)

I used to have a chip on my shoulder,
When it came to the origin of the U.S. of A.
Regarding the birth of this great nation.

"This used to be Mexico", I told a Native-American,
"By Spanish heritage, California and 5 other states,
Became part of the Mexican territory."

"Oh really?", the Native-American inquired,
"And what was Mexico before the Spaniards?

Instantly my pride was dropped to the floor,
The hairs around my ears and the back of my head,
Felt like shooting straight up into the air.

He was right! This was a free land!
It didn't belong to anybody!
In today's day and age, people from all over,
Have the right to live and settle in America.

One Free One (59)

Moral: Success in life is not just about making money but also blessing people. I had just a few seconds to think about what I was going to do. I remembered when I lost my laptop, my wallet and my bus pass and recovered all three. I chased the man down and I offered him a free book in reward for his honesty.

One Free One (59)

Riding the bus is one of,
The most beautiful things,
That have developed in my life.

I have countless thoughts,
Ideas, experiences, and I can write,
Can't do this while driving.

I was approaching one of,
My admirers, a woman from Rome,
When I was startled by a man who,
Gave me my forgotten bag and umbrella,

I thought for a few seconds,
And I chased him down,
"You just won a free book."
 His reward for caring.

One Good Fight (60)

Moral: If you read my first book "Riding The Bus" you might remember that I told you that I reserved my fighting for the karate ring. When I was in junior high I was punched out by some "pachucos" and shortly thereafter I took up karate, not to fight but to know that I could defend myself if I had to. I learned to ignore such bullies and eventually I was left alone. Unfortunately, my own brother was the only bully I ever had to confront.

One Good Fight (60)

Remember I told you,
That I was one to fight,
With my brain, not with my fist?

Well, I did have one good fight,
With the last person in the world,
I should fight, my own brother.

He was also the biggest bully,
Tore up my clothing,
Called me a pansy for being smart.

Came home one day tired,
Of being pushed around,
By my very own brother.

The bullies at school I ignored,
But he was there, day in day out,
He was out of control.

"I am going to show you that I am a man."
Turned over furniture, punched him on the face,
I'll always regret the day I fought my brother.

One One (61)

Reflection: It is now the year 2012 and in retrospect, I don't believe 2011 was the best year ever. I believe that every year is better than the last. The power of positive thinking is inexhaustible. I am now at the end of December, months away from paying all my debt, excluding my mortgage. 2013 will be better than 2012.

One One (61)

Eleven, two equal digits,
One for you, one for me.
Enough to go around for everyone.

This will be the year that I earn more,
I will save more and give more,
This will be the year of prosperity.

One for me, one for you,
This year, blessings will be doubled,
This will be the best one ever.

It all starts with believing,
Believe that you already won,
Prosperity will come your way.

Will it be easy? Probably not.
There will be challenges,
But "you" can make the difference.

Only Once In A Lifetime (62)

Message: Ok, it is time to get a spare key for both of our cars. We have neglected getting another key because they are digital and probably very expensive. At this point I have to look at the practicality of this issue not the money. One time I drove away with both keys, this time I rode away with both keys in my pocket on the bus.

Only Once In A Lifetime (62)

Wow, what can I say?
This should happen only once,
But it has happened to me twice.

People forget things all the time,
Some things important, others not as much,
It is human to make mistakes.

The big wooden key by the door,
Ignored by it's owner, me,
The place to hang the car keys.

Too often I forget to do something so simple,
The giant wooden key by the door,
No spare key for either car.

Time to get smart, I have to remember,
To hang the keys by the door, or my wife might,
Hang me next to the big wooden key by the door.

Paying Attention (63)

Message: Most of us are guilty of texting, dialing numbers or answering our cell phone while driving. People say that students have short attention spans. While these statements may be facts, the truth is that we may be paying attention to something else. The bus driver challenged me to write a poem for him and our conversation became the source of my inspiration. He stopped the bus at my destination without my having to remind him.

Paying Attention (63)

A teacher may say to a student,
"You need to pay attention."
A parent might say to his child,
"Pay attention when I am talking."

You got in an accident
Not because you weren't paying attention,
The truth is you were paying attention
To your cell and the incoming text.

Several times I have missed
My bus stop due to sleeping,
Paying attention to a conversation,
Or just day dreaming.

The driver was paying attention.
He stopped the bus and reminded me,
That I had arrived at my stop.
This poem is in honor of his paying attention.

Piano For Cleaning (64)

Reflection: It is difficult growing up poor, growing up without a father. Poverty and a missing father was no excuse for me. At a very early age I knew I had to struggle and that I would come out ahead. Guess what? I am 56 years old now and I still think I am going to come out ahead. I am still telling people my sad story and asking people for money. As to my missing father, read my first book: Riding The Bus. You'll see that I have had 5 fathers.

Piano For Cleaning (64)

I walked up to the door,
Knocked on the door,
And enunciated my usual spiel.

"Hello, my name is Luis Villalobos,
I am poor, I am 12 years old,
And I have no father."

"I am willing to cut your grass,
Clean your house or do your windows,
I want to go to college when I grow up."

Two elderly ladies came to the door,
"Sorry, we are poor too,
We don't have any money.

We are piano teachers, but,
If you clean our house once a week,
We will give you free piano lessons.

I accepted and for two years,
I had private lessons like the rich kids,
And no one really knew I was poor.

Picking tomatoes (65)

Message: Recently a movie called "A Better Life" came out. The movie depicts the struggles that immigrants may encounter when coming to the United States. Many immigrants who come from Latin America land jobs that require physical labor in the city or in the countryside. My family ended up working under the coldest, hottest dirties conditions, with little pay: farm labor.

Picking tomatoes (65)

My parents moved to the U.S.
In search of a better life,
We left our lives in Tijuana,
For farm life in the Central Valley.

Early in the morning,
Nearly freezing temperatures,
By mid-day and afternoon,
The scorching heat would send,
Rows of sweat down my back.

"¡Apúrate!" Spanish for hurry up,
I would feel a piercing pinch,
On my arm, her fingernails,
Sharp as nails, digging into my skin.

Ten year old boy living,
The life of a grown man.
But there is always a good side,
To a sad story, I remember,
The delicious taste of tomatoes,

Soothing and quenching my thirst.

Priceless (66)

Message: Dreamers are people who make things happen. They believe in the impossible, thus making the impossible possible. In this poem I share with you some of the dreams that became a reality and those that are yet to come. I grieve over people who seemingly have it made in life. I grieve, for example for Lindsay Lohan, who traded places with her mother in "Freaky Friday".

Priceless (66)

I boarded the bus,
And a terrible stench,
Hit me on the face.

I was on the phone,
Trying to balance myself,
With luggage on rollers.

A man screaming,
At the top of his voice,
In the back of the bus.

A woman at the front,
Fidgeting her hands and feet,
In every direction.

To my surprise a conversation emerged,
Between the unsettled,
Woman and the loud man.

The loud man turns to all passengers,
   "You're all half as crazy as this woman."
A priceless bus ride, one of a kind.

Procrastination 2 (67)

Message: It seems funny to me that I am about to publish my second book of inspirational poetry, but I am still procrastinating. It goes to show that life is a struggle and we will never be perfect. I have to remind myself that I must do the little things that weigh so much in the long run. This is Riding The Bus 2, *The Sequel*, therefore this is the sequel to "Procrastination" in my first book.

Procrastination 2 (67)

Although I did not procrastinate,
And I did publish my first book,
I am still procrastinating in small things,

Lose a dollar here, five there, ten,
It all adds up in the end,
Better 20 dollars in than out.

Wait to the last minute,
To prepare a sack lunch,
Spend 20 dollars to eat out.

Wait to send in for the rebate,
Lose the form, forget about it,
Better money coming in than out.

That's it! No more procrastination,
I know I have to do the little things too,
I am going to do them from this moment on.

Quiet (68)

Message: The concept of stopping, waiting, patience often arises in my poetry. It is important to slow down in life, especially if you are always busy. Sometimes it is good to do nothing, just relax and think. I took some time off from my poetry, just to think. Now I have rested enough and I feel inspired to start writing again.

Quiet (68)

It's been a while now,
Since I picked up my lucky pen,
To write a few verses.

It's been a quiet, calm few weeks,
Haven't been running as much,
Just walking to the bus stop.

I've had time to think again,
To stop and thank God,
To assess my triumphs and challenges.

Quiet, think, relax, socialize a little,
Not even selling my chocolates,
Calm, taking my naps.

Perhaps it is time to start writing again.
But I am going to be calm and collected.
Stop, don't haste, just appreciate.

RDD (69)

Message: Racism is another subject that I like to touch upon while riding the bus. Depending on what part of Southern California, the colors will change according to the community. As I ride the 76 I'll see mostly Asian people. When I take the 252 I will see mostly Hispanics. If I go to South LA I will see mostly African-Americans. It is clear that people segregate themselves.

RDD (69)

ADD is an illness,
The victim, can't keep still,
A disorder that impairs,
A person's ability to concentrate.

I propose another illness.
RDD: Racial Deficit Disorder,
The inability to accept others,
To reject people for their race.

There is medication for ADD.
There should be a pill for RDD too,
To calm the rage, the bigotry,
To open the hearts of people.

Racism is stupid.
It doesn't make sense.
Especially, when two people of different,
Cultures, declare their unfailing love.

Recycle Bus (70)

Message: When riding the bus a person can either become very compassionate or very disgusted when observing the poverty in our city. I have seen people get on the bus with humongous suitcases, bags, carts (I'm one of them) but never a man with two large garbage bags filled with recyclables. The man had to go in through the back door, he couldn't fit through the front.

Recycle Bus (70)

A man boarded the bus,
With two large recycle bags,
People could barely walk by.

They were filled with,
Crushed cans and plastic,
A poor man's treasure.

I wonder how this man,
Ever came to this point,
Was he forced to ride the bus?

What was his life like,
As a boy, as a teenager?
Was he now homeless?

What impelled this man,
To turn my luxurious limo,
Into a recycle bus?

Red, Green, Yellow (71)

Reflection: As president of EFIST International I have had the pleasure of meeting several wise and generous people. These giving people take time out of their schedule to talk to my students and encourage them to accomplish goals in life. Cesar, now my friend, earned the right to a personal poem thanks to his knowledge and caring.

Red, Green, Yellow (71)

Remember I told you that,
Wisdom is everywhere?
An old man's gray hair,
Is his mark of wisdom.

Cesar, an avid supporter of EFIST,
Shared this concept with my students,
Life is like a traffic light,
Stop, go, proceed with caution.

Red is for those things,
We should not do,
Drugs, fight, dangerous sex,
Steal, lie, gossip, meddle.

Green is for those things,
That we should do, take medicine,
Fight for your country, get married,
Have children and help others.

Yellow is for those things,
You are not yet quite ready for,
Get married, have sex, not sure,
So wait until the light turns green

Relaxing (72)

Message: Studies have shown that driving can increase stress in a person and often times it may lead to road rage. Although riding the bus is not perfect, just like anything else in life, leaving the driving to someone else may have its benefits. On the bus I can continue writing my poetry and when I get sleepy it is time for a nap. Driving steals away the opportunity to have cool, healthy walks in the morning. No more urges to stop for coffee and a donut.

Relaxing (72)

Never thought riding the bus
Could be so peaceful and relaxing.

When I used to drive,
I would often fall asleep.
I would stop and rest,
Or buy a coffee and a donut.

Now I read and write a little.
When I get sleepy,
I close my comp book,
And put away my "lucky pen".

One time I overslept,
The bus took me to downtown L.A.
Best think that could ever happen,
I woke up so relaxed!

Riding High (73)

Message: "Riding High", I believe, is one of the epic poems of Riding The Bus 2 – *The Sequel*. A young man who was sitting in the back seat blowing carbon dioxide and marijuana fumes into the air conditioner inspired me to write this poem. I was sitting towards the back observing my next poem.

Riding High (73)

No, it's not what you are thinking,
Though that probably happens too,
I am talking about those new Foothill busses,
That have two steps and one more step,
To the third tier at the back of the bus.

Riding high, looking down at everyone,
Seeing eye to eye at big rig drivers,
A good comfortable feeling,
Of peace and tranquility,
My son thought it was cool.

Riding high at the back of the bus,
All for 2 dollars and 45 cents,
Not a worry in my mind,
I know I am saving money,
I am paying off all my debt.

Riding high, higher than limos,
Higher than Jaguars, Lamborghinis,
Mercedes, BMW's, limited editions,
I want to ride high through life,
Owing nothing to no one.

Riding The Bus 2 (74)

Message: In order for things to happen you should never give up, the dreamer should never stop dreaming. Sometimes it is not enough to publish the first book but the second as well. The same mistakes are not repeated, only new ones. Like the bunny from the Duracell batteries commercial, people should also keep going and going until the dream unfolds.

Riding The Bus 2 (74)

I have barely finished my first book,
And I am already giving birth
To Riding The Bus 2. *The Sequel*.

My LUCKY PEN just keeps going,
And going like a Duracell battery.
Words flowing like a fountain.

The miracle unfolding,
Like a never ending story,
Of hope, faith and dreams.

Sharing my books with hopefuls,
Recovered drug addicts,
Looking for a way out.

Riding the bus of life,
Following the path I must,
To bless the countless I meet.

Rise (75)

Message: I believe that working hard and earning one's living, literally, with the sweat of one's forehead is one of the most honorable jobs. Unfortunately such jobs are the lowest paying jobs in the world. Many people who work under such conditions dream of getting out and acquiring a better life style for themselves and their future families.

Rise (75)

My parents brought me to the U.S.
To pick tomatoes, to plow the fields,
At age 10, in the hot sun, sweating,
Wondering, thinking, why I couldn't,
Be in school like the rich kids.

From the very start, I embraced knowledge,
I knew I could do better, grow, improve.
My parents saw the U.S. as a better life,
Better education, more opportunities,
Unfortunately, too many don't seize the moment,

As I grew older, I committed myself,
To books, high school, college, finally,
I became the teacher I dreamed I would be,
Through the years I've had the occasion,
To teach the children of farm workers.

When I moved to Los Angeles,
I gave my students a letter that,
Concluded with these awakening words,
"We shall rise from the cultivation of the fields,
To the harvesting of the professional world."

Shape Of A Gun (76)

Moral: We humans are very opinionated and we have something to say about everyone. It is easy to pass judgment, and how easy it would be to fall into the same trap ourselves. Judging hurts you and others. When someone is going through a hard time the last thing he/she needs is to be judged. We need to help people who are going through problems, in stead of judging them.

Shape Of A Gun (76)

The Bible says, "Judge not,
Lest you be judged".
I'm sure other Holy books,
Warn of judging others.

Next time you judge someone,
Imagine pointing with your finger,
Three fingers are pointing back,
One pointing towards the heavens.

Your hand is in the shape of a gun,
You are killing the hopes and dreams,
Of someone subject to human frailty.
Someone who made the mistake you did.

It's funny how we have said,
"I'll never do that".
While in the future you'll find,
Yourself doing that, and much more.

She Cried (77)

Message: "Everything is relative", Albert Einstein once said. While many children may have warm memories of their grandmothers, a few may remember an abusive, selfish person. As a child I couldn't understand how a father could abandon his children to go take care of his mother. Now that I am older, I understand and I forgive my father and my grandmother. I wonder though, if I will ever cry for her.

She Cried (77)

"My grandmother died", I told her,
Tears coming down her cheeks,
Little did she know that I hated,
The grandma who took my father away.

When my father and mother fought,
I remember him saying he was going,
Back to Mexico to care for his mother,
Who will take care of me I thought?

She cried for a total stranger,
She cried the tears buried in me,
My French teacher, a special person,
I think in loved her more than grandma.

The funeral came in my hometown, Tijuana,
Six children, my mother and father,
The seventh child, me, stayed home,
To this day I never shed a tear for grandma.

Sign Of The Cross (78)

Message: Public transportation is saturated with people with mental illness. These people obviously cannot drive due to their mental state. On the bus and trains you often see people who talk to themselves, ill tempered, those laughing endlessly. This time a man was demonstrating a nervous tension. This man trembled as he continuously made the sign of the cross.

Sign Of The Cross (78)

You see all kinds of stuff on the bus.
I said it once and I'll say it again.
It's amazing the gamut of people you see.

A man was sitting across form me,
Who continuously made the sign of the cross,
And older man, probably in his 70's.

The sign of the cross came continuously,
Less than one minute apart.
I was marveled by his tenacity.

What was he thinking about?
Why was he so scared?
Was he announcing the end of time?

A few traditional Catholics do the sign,
When they go past a Catholic Church, not this man,
Every chance he got, The Sign of the Cross.

Silent (79)

Message: We live in a world where emotional, psychological, physical and sexual abuse have become a way of life. Too many people have come out to confess that they were abused. Recently, priests, pastors, teachers and parents have been exposed as abusers. If you have been hurt, it is time to tell someone and get the help you so deserve.

Silent (79)

I choose to stay silent,
The gory details of abuse,
The secrets held in a child's mind,
Sexual, mental, physical abuse.

How many people choose,
To keep it all inside,
Never tell, try to forget,
Imagine it never happened.

But it did and it hurts,
Innocence wiped away,
Your countenance hiding,
The pain that lurks within,

The time has come to speak up,
To ask for the help you need,
You did not provoke him/her,
The victim must be the victor.

Sitting On A Bench (80)

Message: One of the things I enjoy so much about riding the bus is those quiet, waiting moments. I have time to reflect, to think about the present and plan for the future. Especially on beautiful morning, such as this one, I can just sit there and think. In today's hustle and bustle I don't think people have the time or take the time to just sit and relax.

Sitting On A Bench (80)

Sitting on a bench,
On a bright sunny day,
Overlooking the hills,
Surrounding Cal State LA.

A peaceful feeling came over me,
Confirming my decision to sell my car.
Enjoying the scenery at bus stop 256.
Waiting patiently without any cares.

Sitting on a bench,
Thinking about my decision,
To save money, to ride the bus,
To skip the bumper to pumper stress,

Delicious morning air,
The smell of flowers and trees,
Sitting, relaxing, enjoying,
A decision I will never regret.

Sleeping On The Bus (81)

Reflection: While relaxing, resting, thinking, daydreaming and dozing off I have missed my bus stop. Being able to close my eyes when I am sleepy and tired is invaluable. Driving was such a tedious ordeal for me, just trying to stay awake.   On the bus I can write a little, sleep a little, chat a little and go back to sleep. I just have to remember to put the alarm on my phone so that I won't sleep through my bus stop.

Sleeping On The Bus (81)

It's happened to me more than once,
Sleeping through my bus stop.
Like I said before, sleeping on the bus,
The best thing about riding the bus.

When I used to drive,
I would often fall asleep,
At the wheel, endangering,
My life and the life of others.

I love it when I can close my eyes,
When I am tired and my eyes are heavy.
I love waking up to write my thoughts,
In free-verse style poems.

If I tried to write while driving,
Who knows what kind of accident,
I would have imposed on other drivers?
I feel sleepy now, I think I'll take another nap.

Snoring (82)

Reflection: This creation is one of those funny poems. I am reminded of my poem "Smells" in Riding The Bus, *saving money, dreams and inspiration*. Although many thought the snoring was really funny, I envied the man. He must have felt really relaxed. I wonder if the cinematographer ever put his work of art on YouTube. I think I'll look it up.

Snoring (82)

9:39, just after a football game,
Several people on the bus napping,
Several snoring but one noticeably loud.

Young man across from him taking videos,
Excellent YouTube material, I'm sure,
9:44 pm, man still snoring.
Wakes up a few seconds
And goes back to his preoccupation.

I could say, "Now I've seen it all."
Snoring so hard, he had a captive audience.
People laughing and commenting.

But I wonder how he felt,
Was he relaxed after his symphony?
Like a time clock, he wakes up,
Just before his stop, 9:50 pm.

Now I am beginning to feel sleepy,
My eyes are getting heavy,
Who will laugh at me?
When I let out a big snore?

Son At The Bus Stop (83)

Reflection: When I sold my Tacoma and I started to depend on public transportation, I entered a new paradigm. I began to perceive the world from the perspective of those who are bound to public transportation. I realized that I had a choice: either to love the bus or hate the bus. Looking at my son, waiting at the bus stop I realized that I had to be positive. Picking up my son to go to violin lessons made me feel proud; I had to love the bus too.

Son At The Bus Stop (83)

My son is growing up,
Becoming more confident.
This financial crunch.
Will work for the best in the end.

Before the economic downfall,
My children had two chauffeurs,
My wife was not working, out of the home.
We drove our children everywhere.

My children are learning,
What it means to struggle,
The value of work and money,
They see the value of education.

I am riding the bus now, obviously,
Made an appointment to pick up my son,
Yes, I am riding my limo, like a rich man,
As the bus approaches its stop,

I can see my son and his violin.

Student On The Bus (84)

Message: One of my favorite moments on the bus is when I meet a former student. I get to find out what they are up to. I listen to their stories, their next plan. Often times they will give me insight that I can take back to the classroom. I couldn't have this kind of experience in a car.

Student On The Bus (84)

I met one of my students on the bus.
He was off to college, to get a career.
I remembered him sitting in the back of the room.

He was now grown up, ready for the world,
Making plans for his future,
How fast people grow up!
From one day to another, year to year.

Too many students do not have the vision.
They can't see past high school,
But the future will creep up on them.

Student on a bus, going places.
I wonder what happened to the others.
Did some face up to the grim reality,
Of wasted high school years?

Survive/Thrive (85)

Reflection: I propose a new word, "thrivival", a word designed to replace a more mediocre word, survival. I believe most people get stuck in the routine of everyday living. Routine is great and good habits can take an individual down the road of success. Nevertheless, I don't think that success has an end, but in fact, it is endless. There is a danger with becoming complacent with one's situation. I believe that there is always room for improvement.

Survive/Thrive (85)

I was catching up with my sister,
Regarding everyday struggles and routines,
I told her that I did what I had to,
The usual things that help me survive.

I remember her telling me:
"It is not enough to survive,
In life we have to thrive."
I was ready for these words.

It is not enough to teach,
I have to inspire to my students,
Not enough to provide for my family,
I have to help my children reach new heights.

Let's replace the word survive,
With a more eloquent word: thrive.
Life should not be just about survival,
More importantly, let's call it "thrivival".

Take The First (86)

Moral: The fight against bullying continues and it may never stop as long as there are people on earth. One person, one race, one country trying to overpower the other for money, gain or territory. I don't believe in war or violence but sometimes the victim must defend; a country must defend its people.

Take The First (86)

My son came home crying one day,
He no longer wanted to go to school,
Checked his legs, they were all bruised.

"Things are going to change from now on, son",
Called the principal to inform her,
Of the upcoming tournament.

"As you know, my son is a purple belt,
And I can't afford a private school,
My son has my permission to defend himself."

Take the first, then the second,
But when you see the third punch coming,
High block, step forward, jab!, to the nose.

My son came home so excited the next day.
"Dad! Dad! Guess what happened today!,
This kid grabbed me from the neck.

Punched me on the stomach, cheek, the third punch,
I blocked, stepped forward, jabbed him on the nose,
He rolled over on the grass and it was all over".

The Morning (87)

Message: The concept of time, relaxing, and thinking are some of the concepts that appear often in my poems. Riding the bus has afforded me the time to enjoy those moments that others may consider insignificant. Believe me, a fresh morning walk is not insignificant. Sitting on a bench relaxing and just thinking about anything is a jewel. Riding the bus for me is like a stop watch that gives me the time to reflect.

The Morning (87)

Who has time to enjoy the morning?
I do sitting on a bench one fresh morn.
On a beautiful week day.

Hump day, the over-the-hill day,
Watching people walk by,
Busses and cars zooming by.

Time to relax and observe,
A man cutting the lawn behind me,
A man walking in the bushes to pee.

I remember my life, plan my day,
With my feet and legs stretched out.
I remembered when I helped
A man involved in a car accident,

On this very bus bench.

The Two D's (88)

Reflection: Relationships are hard to maintain and develop. One of those relationships that I cherish is my daughter's. When she was little it was so awesome! We took trips together, went for walks and I miss it. Then her little brother was born and we all had to share our time together. As she got older, I became more and more invisible, but I was always there for her.

The Two D's (88)

When my daughter was little,
We used to do a lot of things together,
On the third year, a little brother intervened.

We used to enjoy Daddy's
Weekly spelling and vocabulary test,
We read together, for 20 minutes a day,

I remember taking the Metrolink,
Rode as far as we could go,
Now times have changed.

But my day of glory,
Returned once again, sweet memories,
She needed me and I was there.

I rented a nice car, coasted to the city
Of Laguna Niguel, orientation day at,
Laguna College of Art and Design.

Once again I was her hero,
Dad and daughter sharing a special moment,
The two D's doing the town again.

The World Is My Home (89)

Reflection: Since I started EFIST International (a designated 501 (c) 3 corporation) I have conducted two trips to Europe. I am currently closing my third trip, London, Paris, and Barcelona. It was always my dream to take students on educational trips to other countries. My life was changed when I traveled to Europe when I was a senior in high school. I still remember my trip like it was yesterday.

The World Is My Home (89)

I want to make the world my home.
I want to travel, see the world, but,
I am lugging family, students, and friends along.

I want to see the leaning tower of Pizza.
The Taj Mahal, the Great Wall of China,
The pyramids of Egypt, Chichén Itzá.

I want to change the lives,
Of those who travel with me,
To leave a mark on those I meet.

I want the world to be my home,
A place where barriers are broken,
Where racism and bigotry have no place.

I want to see Jerusalem, the Gaza Strip,
The Garden of Gethsemane, Mount of Olives,
To learn to communicate in their mother tongues.

Time To Part (90)

Message: Since I wrote this poem I have since found my lucky pen. My wife found it under the washing machine. Having found it again, I secured it to my fanny pack thus never losing it again. I realize that there is no such thing as good luck but we do the best we can and pray that everything will work out. Nevertheless, I feel great having found my LUCKY PEN again.

Time To Part (90)

Can it be?
Did I finally lose my lucky pen?
Does my luck run out here on?

Perhaps it is not luck but a blessing.
I hope this is true, because I trust God.
Nevertheless, I am going to miss that pen.

I looked everywhere,
Last I saw it, I was correcting papers.
Maybe it fell out of my fanny pack.

Will I ever see it again?
Perhaps I don't need a lucky pen anymore,
Maybe I should search within.

Maybe I am the lucky one.
Don't necessarily need material things.
Sublime things have much more value.

Time, My Best Friend (91)

Message: Things that are worth anything take time. It requires effort and a bit of strain at times. You just have to stay your ground and continue until the end. Eventually time will become a memory. Therefore, if you are struggling, just stay with your dream because your struggle won't last for ever.

Time, My Best Friend (91)

I have a best friend.
He is always there.
He was there before my birth,
Will be there after I am gone.

If I have a problem,
Time will see me through.
Like a friend that will stick,
Closer to me than a brother.

Time is the ultimate solution.
Remember going through hard times?
They are only memories, they're gone.
Today will also be a memory.

Half hour in the cold,
To board a cold bus,
Four years from now, I will be,
Totally debt free and remember this day.

Tree (92)

Message: Just like the concept of "waiting" and many others, the concept of "losing and gaining" keeps resurfacing. Like the trees that shed their leaves in the fall and blossom in the spring, people need to lose and gain as well. When we lose something and our roots are strong and go deep, we will come back stronger. I'd like to think that I am like the jacaranda highlighted in this poem.

Tree (92)

I stood at the bus stop,
Contemplating the humongous jacaranda,
Wondering how deep its roots went.

Standing firm through the four seasons,
Losing it's leaves in the fall,
And growing them back in the spring.

I thought of myself,
Standing firm on the ground,
How deep do my roots go?

What will I gain after I lose?
Will I stand in times of hardship?
Will my roots bring back prosperity?

Deeply planted roots, Jack and me,
When spring comes around,
I will be totally debt free.

Trusting (93)

Reflection: There are many times in my life when I am not sure if things will work out. It is during those times that I need someone stronger than me. As I said before my poems are not meant to be religious, I am just sharing myself, candidly with all of you. My truly spiritual poems are reserved for my fifth book, "Riding The Bus, *with Jesus*".

Trusting (93)

"How are you doing", I was asked.
As we crossed paths.
"Trusting in the Lord", I answered.
What else can I do?
What else should I do?

It all begins with trusting God.
Some things we just can't control.
It all ends with trusting God,
Whether things work out or not,
We have to trust in the Lord.

My poems are not necessarily religious,
But what else can I write about,
Except those things that I know,
What else "should" I write about,
Except these things that I believe.

Alcoholics Anonymous has a Higher Power,
The Muslims worship Ala,
There are many Asian religions,
The Jews worship the one True God,
I have a Lord too, his name is Jesus.

Two Choices (94)

Reflection: It is true that things don't always work out the way we expected. A different outcome is no reason to give up. Perhaps you have to approach the problem from a different angle. Maybe your goal is one that takes years to accomplish. The important thing is to stay positive through it all.

Two Choices (94)

If you feel there is no hope,
Change the playing ground.
Change the players and the rules.
You might be successful at something else.

If your plans are not working out,
Make other plans that can succeed.
How do you know it won't work?
Maybe the next one is the one.

If you want to do something,
Keep saying that it will happen,
Keep doing things to make it happen.
Reality happens when dreams come true.

So in life, you have two choices,
You can be positive or,
You can be positive.
If you choose anything else, it's on you.

Under Construction (95)

Message: In my early 20's I remember a t-shirt that read PBPWMGINFWMY. The idea was that people never really finish changing and improving. Life is a journey with many twists and turns. It takes time and effort to change and improve. The acronym means, "PLEASE BE PATIENT WITH ME, GOD IS NOT FINISHED WITH ME YET".

Under Construction (95)

The freeway at the 10/605 junction,
Is under construction, to add a carpool.
My life is also under construction,
Tearing down old bridges and roads,
Building new and stronger, better ones.

It's interesting how it is working out,
The projected completion of the freeway,
Is approximately three years from today,
11/18/13 is the projected debt-free date,
I couldn't have planned it better.

Tearing down old roads, room for a carpool,
Making the freeway wider, better.
Riding my bus, saving on monthly car payments,
Insurance, parking, stress, accidents, car maintenance,
Riding towards a debt free life style.

The projected completion of the carpool lane,
And my debt-freedom miraculously coincide,
Car pool drivers will have more freedom,
And I will be free from financial worries,
I will be there when they cut the ribbon.

Wetbacks (96)

Message: Among the weirdest things I have observed on the bus is the display of racism. Bus 76 is predominately Asian and Asians carry the stereotype that they are loud and rude. Of course, such a statement is not true. I have met very quiet Asians and very polite. Obviously the rude man in this poem is suffering from some kind of mental illness.

Wetbacks (96)

Two Asian passengers got on,
At a stop that was discontinued,
There was a sign to that effect,
Driver informed them of the change.

A third party screams,
From the back of the bus.
"They are wetbacks. They can't read.
They can't even speak English!"

Oh, it gets better, the disrespectable man,
Walks to the front of the bus,
Where the two passengers are sitting,
Had an arduous argument with the driver.

Who hurt this man so deeply,
That he became a bigot?
Why did his life degrade in this way?
Is he past the point of no return?

What Can You See? (97)

Message: I am very proud to say that one of my readers liked my first book so much that she requested a poem for her son. Her son is going through a difficult time where he is losing sight in one eye and a divorce at the same time. The burden has been so overwhelming that he has also lost his faith in God. Losing in life can also be a source of gain. Two of my disabled students live lives as normal people. They are positive students who won't let their disability become a disability but an ability to do things better.

What Can You See? (97)

We are all born
With the gift of health and illness.
Some are born with spinal bifida,
And are bound to a wheelchair.

Others are born with loss of sight.
Their lives are bound for life,
To a human or canine companion,
And a thin long stick with a red tip.

But I know two winner students,
One rolls through life like a pro,
The other sees a world of dreams,
He is the voice of the Wilson Mules.

Some lose their physical attributes,
When they're older, due to an accident,
Losing your feet can take you places,
Losing your sight can show you

Things you never imagined.

What Ever It Takes(98)

Reflection: It has always been a problem for me to motivate my students to work up to their fullest potential. I say this because I have high standards and I want to do something big. I love French like you wouldn't believe. I owe much of this feeling to my French-Basque father who I believe saved me from drugs, gangs and violence.

What Ever It Takes (98)

"What ever it takes",
Read the license plate advertisement.
Of my brand new 97 Toyota Camry.

I took the advertisement,
Off the license plate,
And placed it in front of my classroom.

I initiated my first ever,
Irregular Verb Conjugation Contest.
80 % of the class 80 % on the test was the motto.

I told my students:
"What ever it takes."
"You will learn because you can."

A miracle happened.
More that 80 percent of my students
Earned more than 80 percent on the test!

My students became irregular verb experts.
Many got over 90 percent and could
Write, spell, translate over 350 irregular verbs!
Now, how will I get them to speak?

Why Worry? (99)

Message: Worrying about things doesn't make it any better. Whether a problem has a solution or not worrying will not make the problem better or worse. Some problems have solutions while others may not have resolution. We need "wisdom to change the things we can, accept the things we cannot change and the wisdom to know the difference".

Why Worry? (99)

Will there be enough money?
Will my students excel?
Will my children be successful?
Worrying will not change anything.

Will tomorrow be a better day?
Will my problems go away?
Will my books sell as expected?
Worrying will not make things better.

Will the economy improve?
Will I get laid off from work?
Will this year be better than the last?
Worrying will not improve anything.

If your problem has a solution,
Then why should you worry?
If there is no hope in sight,
Then, why worry?

Woman Singing (100)

Reflection: Mental illness is a big problem. Many go unnoticed until they explode. In the last 20 years there have been several killings by gunman who were obviously mentally ill. When the economy fell many heads of household opted to kill their families and commit suicide. I wonder what will happen to this singing woman if she never recovers from her illness.

Woman Singing (100)

I walked up to the bus stop,
To find a woman singing,
Songs about Mexican chivalry.
Occasionally she would stop,
To profane the name of God.

There are a lot of people,
In need of psychiatric help,
You meet many of these on the bus,
People talking to themselves,
Flaunting what they did in prison.

We boarded the bus,
She continued singing aloud,
Glancing at her with my peripheral vision,
A quick peek, you knew something was wrong,
Stops for a moment only to complain about God,

I wonder about her life, her childhood,
What has she endured to go this far,
Was she abused by a neighbor,
Neglected by her parents?
Complaining, singing, she road on...

You Can Do All Things (101)

Reflection: As I mentioned in my first book of the series Riding The Bus, I cannot exclude my faith from my poems if I am going to be sincere. Neither will I say that my book is exclusive to the spiritual world because I believe that everyone exercises faith in one form or another. I am now riding the Gold Line from China Town to the Atlantic Station in East Los Angeles. I have faith that the train will take me to my destination. It takes faith to move from point A to point B.

You Can Do All Things (101)

You can do anything,
The Bible says.
You just have to ask,
And do it by faith.

Ask to make a difference,
In someone's life,
A person looking for a purpose,
Someone looking for a way out.

God will give you the strength,
To do what you have to do.
It won't be easy, ask for help,
Ask for strength and wisdom.

You can do all things,
Through Christ who strengthens you,
Through He who offers you,
The power and might to succeed.

You Will Go Far (102)

Message: My seventh grade teacher was very influential in my early academic years. She believed in me and told me so several times. She was instrumental in my receiving the Student of the Month Award. I believe it is important to look back only to see all that you have accomplished. Imagine how much more you can accomplish for the remainder of your life.

You Will Go Far (102)

"If you use your brain you,
Will go far in this world", said Miss Nagasaki,
When I turned in one of my short stories.

Of my own volition I often took,
My 7th grade vocabulary words for the week,
And forcedly used all the words in a story.

I occasionally joke around,
When I remember her words,
I wish I could see Miss Nagasaki again.

To tell her, "You know? You were right,
When you said I would go far in this world.
I'm going so far, I haven't gotten there yet."

Today as an older man I remember,
Her words and other words of encouragement,
When I have a dream to keep, a goal to pursue.

Luis Pástor Villalobos

Endorsements

We truly enjoyed reading Luis' first book and we most certainly endorse his second book of inspirational poetry.
Elsa Petty: Escrow Officer
James Petty: Ret. Supervising Dep. Probation Officer

We read Luis' first book and we liked it. We recommend his poetry so be sure to read his first and second book. His poetry can be very useful in everyday living.
Sergio Villalobos and Maria Villalobos
Musician

When I first started high school, I did not know how to deal with it. The first class I went to was your class, my F.A.S. class. I did not know what to expect, but you were a nice teacher with a lot of spirit. I wondered if all teachers were just like you, so I became confident and took in all the new experiences in high school with no fear. I liked how you would read us some of your poems because they were really inspirational.
Dennys Ramirez: Class of 2013 – The Prominent Class

Other reasons why I appreciate you is how you give the best advice. With the book you wrote you were able to send messages with each poem. It was helpful and inspiring being able to listen to a new poem every day. Thank you for all the assistance in high school with your help I feel prepared to experience college.
Juan Gonzalez – MBA Delegate – Class of 2013

I will never forget all the fun activities you included in your class to enhance learning. I especially loved how you always read us a poem at the beginning of the class period to make us feel more related to you and your bus experiences.
Jennifer Gudino – Class of 2013 – The Prominent Class

Riding The Bus 2 – *The Sequel*

Luis Pástor Villalobos

CONCLUSION

If you are reading this conclusion you may have already gone through most of the poems in my second book of free-verse story poems, perhaps my first book Riding The Bus1 too. You may have discovered that your life is not much different from that of others. We all have dreams and aspirations. There are things that we want to do in our lifetime that require much dedication. Hopefully you understood that dreams can come true.

Now I want to say thank you. Thank you for holding this book in your hand. Let it transcend from your finger tips to your palms and lodge deep in your heart. Share your favorite poems on social media, share them with your closest friends. Please help me accomplish my dream to hold a motivational speech, maybe through TedTalks or maybe address a Fortune 500 corporation.

Now go out and conquer your dreams. Set high goals, you may not reach them all but certainly you will have covered much ground. Don't give up just because you reach an obstacle. I believe that the obstacles in life mark the path we must follow. So now, walk confidently up and down, side to side those stepping stones that are the only way to success, but don't do it alone, maybe you can ask Jesus to go along with you.

Luis Pástor Villalobos

ABOUT THE AUTHOR

Mr. Luis Pastor Villalobos is married and is a father of two children. He and his family have lived in the city of Baldwin Park, California for a little over 10 years. He has been teaching for 25 years and has been at Woodrow Wilson High School in El Sereno for the past seven years. Mr. Villalobos earned his Bachelor of Arts in French and a minor in Spanish at California State University, Stanislaus. He earned his teaching credential at California State University, Dominguez Hills, cleared his Spanish credential at California State University, Los Angeles and his French credential at California State University, San Bernardino. Mr. Villalobos is also certified to teach CAHSEE Math and English. He continued his education at the University of Life and earned a master's and a PhD as a father and a husband ☺. His dedication to his family has paid off. His daughter Tanya Celeste, 19, will be a junior at Parsons The New School, studying fashion design. His son Luis Alberto, 15, will be a junior at Los Angeles County High School for the Arts and he is currently at Meadowmount School of Music in Westport, New York. Mr. Villalobos' greatest dream is to continue inspiring others to follow and accomplish their own dreams.

Luis Pástor Villalobos

Made in the USA
Columbia, SC
04 June 2025